JOSEPH PULITZER

and the Story behind the Pulitzer Prize

GREAT ACHIEVEMENT
A·W·A·R·D·S

Mitchell Lane
PUBLISHERS

P.O. Box 196
Hockessin, Delaware 19707

GREAT ACHIEVEMENT
A·W·A·R·D·S

Titles in the Series

Visit us on the web at www.mitchelllane.com
Comments? Email us at mitchelllane@mitchelllane.com

JOSEPH PULITZER
and the Story behind the Pulitzer Prize

GREAT ACHIEVEMENT
A·W·A·R·D·S

Printing   3   4   5   6   7   8   9

Library of Congress Cataloging-in-Publication Data
Zannos, Susan.
     Joseph Pulitzer and the story behind the Pulitzer Prize / Susan Zannos.
          p. cm. — (Great achievement awards)
     Summary: A biography of Joseph Pulitzer and the story of his creation of the Pulitzer Prizes.
     Includes bibliographical references and index.
     ISBN 1-58415-179-X (library bound)
     1. Pulitzer, Joseph, 1847-1911—Juvenile literature. 2. Journalists—United States—Biography—Juvenile literature. 3. Pulitzer Prizes—Juvenile literature.   [1. Pulitzer, Joseph, 1847-1911. 2. Journalists. 3. Pulitzer Prizes.]   I. Title. II. Series.
     PN4874.P8Z36 2003
     070.92—dc21
     [B]
     2002011059

ABOUT THE AUTHOR: Susan Zannos has been a lifelong educator, having taught at all levels, from preschool to college, in Mexico, Greece, Italy, Russia, and Lithuania, as well as in the United States. She has published a mystery *Trust the Liar* (Walker and Co.) and *Human Types: Essence and the Enneagram* (Samuel Weiser). Her book *Human Types* was translated into Russian in 2003, and Susan was invited to Russia to tour and lecture about her book. Another book she wrote, *Careers in Education,* (Mitchell Lane) was selected for inclusion in the New York Public Library's "Books for the Teenage 2003 List." She has written nearly twenty books for children and young adults, including *The Life and Times of Franz Joseph Haydn* and *Cesar Chavez* (Mitchell Lane). Susan lives in Oregon House, California.

PHOTO CREDITS: Cover: Hulton/Archive; p. 6 Barbara Marvis; p. 9 Barbara Marvis; p. 12 Hulton/Archive; p. 15 Museum of the City of New York/Corbis; p. 18 Hulton/Archive; p. 22 The Pulitzer Foundation; p. 24 The Pulitzer Foundation; p. 26 Barbara Marvis; p. 30 Hulton/Archive; p. 32 Hulton/Archive; p. 34 Barbara Marvis

PUBLISHER'S NOTE: The following story has been thoroughly researched and to the best of our knowledge represents a true story. Documentation of such research is contained on page 46.

     The web sites referenced in this book were all active as of the publication date. Because of the fleeting nature of some internet sites, we cannot guarantee they will be active when you are reading this book.

TABLE OF CONTENTS

The Statue of Liberty stands tall and proud on the 89-foot pedestal built with $100,000 raised by Joseph Pulitzer's crusade in the New York World.

LIBERTY

The people of France wanted to offer a special gift, a magnificent monument to help the American people celebrate the centennial of their Declaration of Independence. In 1875, almost one hundred years after the beginning of the American Revolutionary War, one of France's finest sculptors, Auguste Bartholdi, began work on a statue that would symbolize liberty.

Bartholdi enlisted the help of Gustave Eiffel, the structural engineer who would later build the famous Eiffel Tower in Paris, to build the framework that would support the monument to liberty. They selected Bedloe's Island, which would later be named Liberty Island, in New York Harbor as the site for the statue. The 150-foot monument, constructed of 250,000 pounds of steel and over 179,000 pounds of copper, was completed in June of 1884 and presented to America by the people of France on July 4, Independence Day.

But there was a problem: The pedestal on which the monument was to be displayed had not been built. The $100,000 that was needed for the project had not been raised. It seemed as though the magnificent gift from the French people would remain in the 214 crates it had taken to ship it across the Atlantic.

In the *New York World* newspaper on March 16, 1885, the opening editorial had this to say:

It would be an irrevocable disgrace to New York City and the American Republic to have France send us this splendid gift without our having provided even so much as a landing place for it. . . . There is but one thing that can be done. We must raise the money. The *World* is the people's paper, and it now appeals to the people to come forward and raise this money. The $250,000 that the statue cost was paid in by the masses of the French people— by the workingmen, the tradesmen, the shop girls, the artisans— by all, irrespective of class or condition. Let us respond in like manner. Let us not wait for the millionaires to give this money. It is not a gift from the millionaires of France to the millionaires of America but a gift of the whole people of France to the whole people of America.

Take this appeal to yourself personally. . . . Give something, however little. . . .

The publisher of the *World* was Joseph Pulitzer (pronounced by the family as PULL-et-suhr, commonly pronounced as PYOU-let-suhr). He was himself an immigrant, a Hungarian Jew who had arrived in America at the age of seventeen, penniless but eager for adventure. In 1883, when Pulitzer bought the *World,* the daily paper had a circulation of about 11,000. A year later the circulation had more than tripled and was increasing rapidly. Pulitzer had not increased the paper's circulation by taking readers away from the other New York newspapers—he had done it by appealing to the new immigrants (over 5 million had entered the United States during the previous ten years), the working-class people who had not formerly been in the habit of reading newspapers.

The poor people of New York read the *World.* And the poor people of New York donated the money that would place the Statue of Liberty on an 89-foot pedestal on Bedloe's Island. Immigrants who had come into New York Harbor themselves only a few years before now sent whatever they could afford. Sometimes it was only a few cents, sometimes a dollar or two. They may have been poor, but they wanted the symbol of freedom, torch raised high, to welcome the other immigrants who would arrive in the same harbor with the same dreams.

To help with the fund-raising for a pedestal for the Statue of Liberty, Emma Lazarus wrote a poem that would be placed on a bronze plaque at the base of the statue. The famous final lines of the poem have inspired generations of Americans to remember their own immigrant heritage:

Give me your tired, your poor,

Your huddled masses yearning to breathe free,

The wretched refuse of your teeming shore.

Send these, the homeless, tempest-tost to me,

I lift my lamp beside the golden door!

This statue of Emma Lazarus, the poet who wrote the famous lines inscribed on the Statue of Liberty, is on Liberty Island.

In addition to creating the campaign to build the pedestal, Joseph Pulitzer contributed $250 to the fund. Only one man of wealth contributed: Pierre Lorillard gave $1,000. The rest of the $100,000 came from the common people, "the workingmen, the tradesmen, the shop girls, the artisans" to whom Pulitzer had appealed in his newspaper. By August 11, the *World* announced that the goal had been reached—it had collected $100,000 in donations. The pedestal for the Statue of Liberty would be built.

The crusade to collect the money for the pedestal was far from the only one undertaken by Joseph Pulitzer. Some of the *World*'s crusades attempted to uncover corruption in business and government. The newspaper prevented the Louisiana lottery from swindling citizens out of $10 million a year. It proved that Bell Telephone had become a monopoly by fraudulent practices. It revealed that Henry Hilton had turned a home that was supposed to provide a charitable shelter for poor working women into the Park Avenue Hotel, for his own profit. It exposed political corruption wherever it found government practices that harmed the public good.

Many of Pulitzer's campaigns, like the one to raise money for the Statue of Liberty, had charitable goals. The *World* collected $20,000 from its readers to aid Johnstown, Pennsylvania, flood victims. It financed a Free Doctors' Corp for the Sick Babies of the Poor, hiring 35 doctors who treated 12,821 children in one year, from readers' contributions. It gave free Thanksgiving dinners, Christmas trees, and parties to poor children. It discovered that Stuyvesant Park, which was public property, was being used exclusively by the rich, and had it opened to the public. The *World* proposed free lectures, free public baths, and more city parks; it campaigned for better streets, libraries, and art galleries, and more and better schools.

Some of the investigations done by the *World* corrected instances of social injustice. The paper exposed Georgia's slave-gang system of farming and urged reform of the law committing delinquent children to institutions, allowing the children to be returned to their parents. It was instrumental in passing a law requiring women factory inspectors to be hired, and it improved the working conditions of Pennsylvania miners. The paper also persuaded the New York State legislature to change the harsh law that sent debtors to jail.

The *World* also carried on criminal investigations in its columns. It provided evidence used to convict the owners of illegal gambling establishments in New Jersey. It had the warden of a New York City prison dismissed for extortion. It solved a murder case in Connecticut, leading to the conviction of the killer. It helped send contractor Walter Buddensiek to prison for building substandard houses that collapsed soon after the owners moved in.

Joseph Pulitzer changed journalism from what it had been in the nineteenth century to what it would be ever after. He insisted that his reporters and news editors not only report the news, but also make the news. They didn't make news by writing stories that weren't true. Pulitzer was fanatic about accuracy! They made news by revealing what was wrong and crusading to make it right.

Joseph Pulitzer was tall and thin, with a large nose, poor eyesight, and a weak chin, which he concealed by growing a beard.

A Hungarian Jew

In the middle of the nineteenth century, Philip Pulitzer, a wealthy Magyar-Jewish grain merchant, and his Roman Catholic Austrian wife, Louise, began their family in the town of Makó in southeast Hungary. Their first son, Louis, died young. Their second son, Joseph, was born on April 10, 1847. Four years later Joseph's younger brother, Albert, was born, and later his sister, Irma.

Philip Pulitzer was in poor health. In 1853, when Joseph was six years old, his father retired and moved his family to Budapest. Young Joseph was also frequently ill, and his parents hired a tutor for him so that he could study at home. In spite of his bouts of sickness, Joseph was an intense scholar, reading eagerly, learning French and German, and questioning everything he saw or heard or read. The Pulitzer family was well educated and cultured. Young Joseph enjoyed music, theater, and literature. He also became an excellent chess player. Of all the advantages of his privileged upbringing, it was his chess playing that would contribute most to his survival in the difficult life he chose.

Perhaps stories of his fierce Magyar ancestors inspired him to dream of military glory. Whatever it was, young Joseph was determined to be a soldier. He wanted to be a member of the Maria Theresa Division. He liked to watch the changing of the guard at the palace in Budapest. He enjoyed riding and was proud of the fine horse his father gave him.

Joseph grew fast and tall. By the time he was sixteen years old, he was six feet two inches tall, very thin, and physically weak. He had a large hooked nose, a weak chin, and poor eyesight. He was excitable and had difficulty getting along with people because he was so critical. Also, there was anti-Semitism in Hungary, and other boys taunted him for being Jewish. Quite probably they were jealous of his brilliant mind.

While Joseph was still a teenager, his father died. His mother married a Budapest merchant whom Joseph didn't like. He was miserable at home with his new stepfather, so when he was sixteen he decided he would leave home and become a soldier. His mother had two brothers who were officers in the Austrian army. Joseph tried to enlist, perhaps hoping that his uncles would be able to help him. He was rejected because of his youth, his poor eyesight, and his physical weakness.

Even at that early age, Joseph Pulitzer was not one to give up easily. He was determined to find military glory. He went to Paris and tried to enroll in the French Foreign Legion to serve in Mexico, where they defended the right of Archduke Maximilian to the throne. The French did not, however, feel that they needed the assistance of the gangling young Joseph Pulitzer. He continued on to London, where he attempted to enlist in the British army to serve in India. They didn't want him either. In addition to his youth and physical problems, he didn't speak any English.

He had about run out of armies. He went to Hamburg, the busy German port, and tried to ship out as a sailor. No luck there either. In Hamburg, however, he learned of agents who were looking for recruits to fight for the Union Army in the Civil War in America. These agents wanted to earn the federal bounty that would be paid for recruits. Joseph had finally found an army that wanted him. He was soon on a crowded ship crossing the Atlantic. He reached Boston Harbor late in the summer of 1864. He knew the agents would receive money for his enlistment, but he saw no reason why he shouldn't have the money himself. After all, he was the one who was going to be in the army.

The first major land battle of the Civil War, the Battle of Bull Run, took place on July 21, 1861. The many casualties in battles like this caused recruiters to go to Europe to find new recruits like the young Joseph Pulitzer.

Shortly after midnight, while the ship was at anchor in Boston Harbor, Joseph slipped over the side into the cold water. He swam to shore, took a train to New York, and the next day found the recruiting office and a German-speaking soldier who signed him up. Joseph Pulitzer was finally a soldier, a member of the First New York Lincoln Cavalry of the Union Army.

Too late Joseph realized that he had brought calamity upon himself. In his dreams of military glory he had overlooked the fact that a soldier is first and foremost required to follow orders. And if there was one thing he never had been and never would be able to do, it was follow orders. Furthermore, the other recruits tormented him, making fun of his lack of English, his big nose and weak chin, and his disdain for the coarseness of camp life. Neither had he left anti-Semitism behind in Europe. The other soldiers called him "Jewseph," and "Joey the Jew."

At one point a sergeant so enraged him with his taunts about his big nose that Joseph attacked the man. He was very nearly court-martialed, but was rescued by a senior officer who admired Joseph's chess playing. Although Joseph took part in four minor skirmishes, he experienced more conflict and combat with his fellow Union soldiers than with the supposed enemies in the Confederacy. After Lee's surrender to Grant at Appomattox, Joseph Pulitzer rode in the victory parade in Washington on May 23, 1865. After that he soon took his discharge pay and was very glad to leave the military service he had been so determined to enter.

Hard times were far from over. Joseph Pulitzer was just one of hundreds of recently discharged soldiers on the streets of New York City, looking for work. He was at a disadvantage because he didn't speak English. Desperate when his mustering-out pay was gone, he rode the rails to St. Louis, where there was a large German-speaking population and at least he would be able to look for work among people who knew a language he spoke and understood. The freight trains went only as far as East St. Louis—there would be no bridge across the Mississippi in that area until 1874. Pulitzer arrived on October 10, 1865. He had no money for the ferry, so he worked his way across the river by stoking the boiler with coal (a job done to move the ferry across water).

The first job he found in St. Louis was caring for mules, and it only lasted a couple of days. He had come upon creatures as stubborn as himself. Years later he was quoted in the *New York Evening Post* as saying, "The man who has not cared for sixteen mules does not know what work and troubles are." After that Joseph had a series of jobs: deckhand, construction worker, waiter, errand boy. In between jobs he spent his days at the Mercantile Library, studying English and often playing chess. He became known to many of the cultured German citizens of St. Louis, including the editors of the German-language newspaper.

When Joseph finally got a break, it came in the form of seeming misfortune. He paid five dollars to a smooth-talking con man who promised him a good job in Louisiana. With others who were also expecting to be hired, he set off by steamboat down the Mississippi, only to be set ashore and abandoned forty miles downriver. Joseph and the other angry men had to walk back to St. Louis, swearing to do great harm to the man who had deceived them. The man had disappeared by the time they returned, but a reporter suggested that Pulitzer write a story about the incident for the German-language newspaper, the *Westliche Post.* He did. It was his first published news story.

The editors of the paper, Dr. Emil Preetorius and Carl Schurz, were impressed with young Pulitzer's hard work, intelligence, and way with words, as well as with his chess game. They gave him occasional writing assignments for the paper while he pursued several other jobs. One was burying cholera victims and keeping records during an epidemic in the summer of 1866, a job that no one else would do. When the epidemic was over, so was the job. Next he worked for a railroad company securing articles of incorporation from the counties through which the railroad would pass. He did so well at this that he was encouraged to study to become a lawyer.

On March 6, 1867, Joseph Pulitzer became a citizen of the United States. Soon after, his younger brother, Albert, came from Hungary to St. Louis. Albert had the good sense to learn English before coming, and he soon got a job teaching German in a local high school. The following year Joseph was admitted to the bar, but he never had much of a law career. His broken English and odd appearance did not inspire confidence in potential clients.

Meanwhile at the *Westliche Post,* the editors were discussing the need for hiring a new reporter. They were deciding whether to offer the job to a veteran reporter or to young Pulitzer, whom they knew was inexperienced but thought was promising. Their choice was Pulitzer. He said later, "I could not believe it. I, the unknown, the luckless, almost a boy of the streets, selected for such responsibility—it all seemed like a dream."

But it was his life before that had been the dream, a kind of restless nightmare of wandering and trying to figure out what he was supposed to do with his life. When he became a reporter at the age of twenty-one, he awoke to his destiny.

Carl Schurz, editor of the St. Louis Westliche Post, *was Joseph Pulitzer's mentor in both journalism and politics.*

NEWSPAPERMAN

Joseph Pulitzer was so enthusiastic about his new job as reporter for the *Westliche Post* that he frequently worked sixteen hours a day. He would arrive at the newspaper at 10:00 A.M., and sometimes he would still be working at two o'clock the next morning. The long night hours reading and writing in poor light put a strain on his already weak eyesight, but that didn't stop him. The other reporters made fun of his appearance and his determination, just as the soldiers in the army had made fun of him. But he didn't mind as much. He was a reporter, a job that he valued, and that helped him hold his temper.

Young Joseph had found a good mentor in publisher Carl Schurz, an intelligent man with a commitment to democracy. Schurz had an excellent writing style in both German and English, and was an effective speaker who could move his listeners to action. From Schurz, Pulitzer learned the passion for accuracy and brevity in writing that he would insist upon throughout his life. Before long the reporters who had ridiculed Pulitzer were translating his articles into English for their own papers.

Schurz and his partner, Preetorius, introduced their young reporter to the political life of Missouri. He was sent by the paper to the state capital in Jefferson City, where he became familiar with the procedures of the state legislature. Pulitzer's large nose turned out to be a nose for news, particularly news of any shady political dealings.

His efforts to expose anyone who abused the public trust did not make him popular with those who were getting rich at the expense of the people. These efforts did give him a growing reputation as an honest and dedicated journalist.

In December of 1869, Joseph Pulitzer was at a Republican meeting where the leaders were looking for a candidate to fill a legislative vacancy. When their first choice declined, they nominated Pulitzer. He won the election, to his considerable delight. He found that he had a taste for politics as well as for reporting, and now he was in a position not only to expose corruption in the state government, but also to help enact laws that would end it. In one instance, while drafting a bill to reform the County Court, he enraged a powerful man who attacked him physically. In the scuffle that followed, Pulitzer drew a pistol and ended up shooting the man in the knee.

Although Pulitzer was charged with assault and was criticized for the affair, his friends supported him and he was let off with a fine. He continued his fight against corruption in both writing and political action with such zeal that the editors of the *Westliche Post* offered him the opportunity to buy a controlling interest in the paper. He rapidly proved himself a good businessman, buying another German-language newspaper and immediately selling it for its press franchise and machinery. With his profit he was in a position to shop for another newspaper to buy.

A big year for Joseph Pulitzer was 1878. During one of his trips to Washington, D.C., he fell in love with the beautiful and aristocratic Kate Davis. She was related to the leader of the Confederacy, Jefferson Davis, and her family moved in circles of wealth and privilege. These circles did not willingly admit Jews into their families, so Joseph concealed his background until after he and Kate were married on June 19, 1878, in an Episcopal church in Washington. (Her parents were disturbed enough that she was marrying an immigrant with a thick accent.)

Joseph took his new wife on an extended honeymoon to Europe. While there he looked around to see if there might be a newspaper for sale, but he didn't find any. He eventually found one in his own backyard. On December 9, 1878, a failing newspaper in St. Louis went up for auction. It was generally agreed that the *St. Louis Dispatch* was nearly worthless. Joseph Pulitzer was able to buy it for $2,500. He was thirty-one years old, newly married, and now the owner of his own newspaper. The day after Pulitzer bought the *Dispatch,* the owner of the only rival evening newspaper, the *Evening Post,* showed up at the newspaper plant. He suggested that instead of fighting each other for readers, they should merge the two papers. The man's name was John Dillon, and Joseph Pulitzer liked him and shared his political views. Pulitzer agreed to the merger on the condition that he would have control over editorial policy. And thus the *St. Louis Post-Dispatch* was born.

On December 12, Pulitzer's first editorial appeared in the first issue of the newly combined papers: "The POST *and* DISPATCH will serve no party but the people; . . . will oppose all frauds and shams wherever and whatever they are; will advocate principles and ideas rather than prejudices and partisanship."

Among the first crusades to oppose frauds and shams was an attack on those wealthy citizens who falsified their tax returns. Pulitzer published the returns of tax-dodgers, which of course made them furious. Since these were rich and powerful men, they retaliated by withdrawing advertising from the papers. Undaunted, Pulitzer continued the attacks—and circulation grew rapidly.

The newspaper moved to a new building, and Kate and Joseph Pulitzer moved to a new home in the best part of town. Their first son, Ralph, was born in June 1879, and Joseph began staying home on Sundays to be with his family, which was a radical change from his usual workaholic habits. This period was probably the happiest in Pulitzer's life. It was marred only by Kate's fears for his safety because he angered so many people with his crusades against corruption.

In addition to crusades for social causes, the *Post-Dispatch* specialized in stories of crime and violence. Pulitzer was accused of sensationalism. He retaliated by saying, "The press may be licentious, but it is the most magnificently repressive moral agent in the

Joseph Pulitzer (left) with his brother Albert. Albert Pulitzer moved to St. Louis in 1867. He later moved to New York and started his own newspaper, the New York Journal.

world today. More crime, immorality and rascality is prevented by the fear of exposure in the newspapers than by all the laws, moral and statute ever devised." He was quite likely correct, but he also knew that stories about crime, immorality, and rascality would sell newspapers. The circulation of his newspaper continued to climb. His partner, John Dillon, grew tired of the pressure and sold his interest to Pulitzer.

Pulitzer became wealthier and more socially prominent, and his family continued to grow. Daughter Lucille was born in September 1880, and daughter Katherine in June 1882. Then things started to go wrong. The constant pressure of work was weakening Joseph Pulitzer's health. Three-year-old Ralph was also ill. In October the family traveled to Europe in hopes that father and son would recover. While Pulitzer was absent, his managing editor, John Cockerill, shot and killed a man who had stormed into the newspaper's office to object violently to a story Cockerill had written about him.

Pulitzer rushed back from Europe to stand by his editor, but the uproar caused by the event was so intense that he was forced to fire Cockerill, even though the courts found that the editor had acted in self-defense. The prominent members of St. Louis society and the other local newspapers continued to attack Pulitzer, claiming that the violence had been the inevitable result of the sensationalism of the *Post-Dispatch*. The Pulitzers, formerly accepted in high society, were no longer welcome in St. Louis.

Joseph Pulitzer was shaken by the response of the public. Circulation of the *Post-Dispatch* fell, and advertising revenue all but disappeared. He left his former partner, John Dillon, in charge as editor of the paper and headed back to Europe. He never got there.

On his way back to Europe, Joseph Pulitzer stopped in New York to visit his brother, Albert, who had recently started his own newspaper, the *New York Morning Journal*. Albert was not interested in politics or crusading. He was interested in making money, and he did. His paper specialized in entertainment, gossip, and sporting events. It sold for a penny and soon had a large circulation. It was not the sort of thing Joseph was interested in. What Joseph was interested in was hearing that the *New York World*, owned by the infamous robber baron Jay Gould, was for sale.

Pulitzer called on Gould, who was asking over half a million dollars for the nearly defunct newspaper. Albert, and nearly everyone else Joseph talked to, discouraged him from paying so much for a

Joseph Pulitzer met his wife Kate Davis, shown here, in Washington, DC. She was from a wealthy family who would not have approved of her marrying a Jew, so he had to conceal his background until after their marriage.

newspaper so nearly dead. Crushed by his defeat in St. Louis, ill and full of anxiety, Pulitzer returned to the hotel where his family was staying. He told Kate that he had given up the idea of buying the *World* and was ready to sail for Europe.

But Kate Pulitzer knew her husband well. She felt that without a newspaper, his health would continue to suffer, that his passion for journalism was the driving force of his life. She convinced him to try again to make a deal with Gould. This time he succeeded.

The edition of the *World* on May 11, 1883, was the first one published under Joseph Pulitzer's ownership. In a statement that echoed his first *Post-Dispatch* editorial, he pledged to produce a newspaper "dedicated to the cause of the people rather than that of purse-potentates—devoted more to the news of the New than the Old World—that will expose all fraud and sham, fight all public evils and abuses—that will serve and battle for the people with earnest sincerity."

This statue of Joseph Pulitzer stands on Liberty Island near the Statue of Liberty.

THE NEWSPAPER WARS

The first battle that Joseph Pulitzer had to wage after he became owner of the *New York World* was the battle for circulation. He won it. The final Sunday edition under the previous ownership sold 15,770 copies. Two years later, on May 10, 1885, the Sunday *World* sold 153,213 copies—and this was during a period when there were problems with the presses and the newsstands frequently sold out before the demand for papers was satisfied. This was an astonishing record! A tenfold increase in circulation! How had Pulitzer accomplished it?

He used a number of techniques, many of which he had developed at the *St. Louis Post-Dispatch.* He not only introduced methods that made the *World* the most widely read newspaper in America, but in the process he changed the history of journalism. He brought John Cockerill to New York. In spite of the difficulties over the shooting in St. Louis when he had to fire Cockerill, Pulitzer believed him to be the best editor he knew and put him in charge of the *World.*

In St. Louis Joseph Pulitzer had won readers to the *Post-Dispatch* by appealing to the middle class. In New York his battle was for the lower classes. Before 1883 there had been no newspaper that concerned itself with the condition of the immigrants, the sweatshop workers, the urban poor. The literacy rate among the poor was low. Many of the thousands of new immigrants that poured into New York knew hardly any English. The *World* responded with large easy-to-read headlines and lots of pictures. Pulitzer insisted that his reporters use simple vocabulary and sentence structure in their stories.

The *World* was unique in choosing its articles and making its editorial decisions on the side of the masses on all political and social issues. And the masses rewarded Pulitzer with a circulation higher than any American newspaper had ever had before, and by making him a millionaire.

Pulitzer did not invent sensationalism—presenting stories about sex, crime, violence, tragedy, and scandals. But he used sensationalism in ways that were enormously successful. He insisted that the dramatic headlines be backed up with stories containing solid facts. The walls of the newsrooms at the *World* were plastered with posters carrying one command: Accuracy! Accuracy! Accuracy! Any reporter who didn't have the facts soon would be out of a job.

Pulitzer demanded that his writers and editors carry on crusades. Not once a month or once a week, but every single day the paper had to report on the progress of a continuing crusade. It might be a crusade to reveal political corruption, to bring a criminal to justice, to raise money for a hospital, or to improve conditions in prisons, but the *World* always had a crusade going on.

He began the practice of printing a sports page, which was popular with men living and working in the city because they had little chance to participate in sports themselves. He attracted women readers with features on fashion and social life. And he began the tradition of the comic page.

Some aspects of the social and technological developments of the time also contributed to Pulitzer's success. The rapid transit system changed the habits of newspaper readers. Instead of reading in their homes, working people read their papers on crowded trains. The newspapers responded by making the size of the pages smaller so that they would be easier to handle in the crowded cars. Instead of having a subscription to newspapers, people bought them at newsstands near the subway stations. And they were more likely to buy a paper like the *World* that had pictures and bold exciting headlines.

After some initial difficulty keeping up with the demand, the *World* installed new and more powerful presses that could supply as many papers as the people would buy.

As his newspaper grew, so did his family. Although 1884 brought the death of his daughter Katherine, in 1885 his son Joseph Jr. was born, in 1886 his daughter Edith, and in 1888 his daughter Constance. Their father was seldom at home. It was left to Kate to raise the children and preside over their household, although Joseph made all the decisions and tried to control every aspect of family life as he did with his business life.

Unfortunately, Pulitzer was paying a terrible price for his success. His health began failing rapidly. Not only was he working his habitual long hours at his newspaper, but also in 1885 he ran for the U.S. House of Representatives. He won. His efforts to divide his energies between New York and Washington were more than even a healthy man could have managed, and he was not a healthy man. Soon insomnia, indigestion, and a nervous excitability overcame him. Furthermore, he soon realized that he had far more power as a newspaper publisher than he had as a politician. After four months in Congress, he resigned.

As his illnesses grew worse, Pulitzer became more and more difficult. He was never an easy man to get along with, but his insomnia, headaches, asthma, indigestion, and nervous disorders caused him to rage and curse whenever anything did not suit him. And he was able to find fault with nearly everything. He was a tyrant at home, and Kate and the children had to endure his outbursts. At the newspaper office his curses could be heard all over the building. His biographer, William Swanberg, reported that editor John Cockerill said of him, "He was the damnedest best man in the world to have in a newspaper office for one hour in the morning. For the remainder of the day he was a damned nuisance."

The doctors he consulted all told him that he needed complete rest if he wanted to regain his health. But rest was something Pulitzer had never been able to do. He tried, but his efforts to avoid anything connected with either the newspaper or politics only made

William Randolph Hearst bought the New York Journal *from Joseph Pulitzer's brother Albert and began a circulation war with Joseph Pulitzer's* New York World.

him deeply depressed. His insomnia and anxiety increased. He tried traveling, visiting health spas and resorts all over Europe. While he traveled he constantly sent letters and cables back to his newspaper. He had all of the New York papers delivered to him wherever he happened to be, and sent lengthy comments to his editors, making criticisms and giving orders. The staff at the *World* hated to see the mail ships arrive.

Everyone—his doctors, his family, his friends, his editors at the newspapers—told Joseph Pulitzer not to worry. That was like telling him not to breathe. He had built his entire career, newspaper empire, and fortune on worrying over every detail. He couldn't stop. By 1890 he was almost completely blind. He could no longer read even the largest print and could barely tell day from night. As his eyesight failed, his hearing grew more and more acute until it was a constant torment to him. He could not tolerate even the ordinary noises of daily life, so that he could no longer bear to be with his family. The small sounds his children made, even when they tried very hard to make no noise, caused him anguish and pain. His last, and favorite, son, Herbert, was born in 1895. It was Pulitzer's great sorrow that he could not see the boy he loved so dearly.

Pulitzer's tortured life became a constant struggle to find cures for his ailments and to create a silent environment. He had a special structure, a tower of silence with five-foot-thick walls, built on his estate in Bar Harbor, Maine—but he could still hear the foghorns. He had special rooms, completely insulated and with doors running on silent ball bearings, constructed in his New York mansion. Finally, he spent most of his days on his yacht, the *Liberty,* which had coiled rope fastened to the decks to muffle the sounds of the crew's footsteps. Only far out on the world's oceans could he get away from the ordinary sounds of human life.

A staff of secretaries and doctors constantly attended Pulitzer, as well as companions whose job it was to read to him, engage in conversation, and take dictation for the continual stream of letters to his family and his newspapers. No matter where in the world he happened to be, he desperately tried to control every aspect of his personal and business interests.

From 1896 through 1898, Joseph Pulitzer waged the most shameful battle of his life and came close to losing everything of value that he had acquired. This battle was the circulation war with multimillionaire William Randolph Hearst. Hearst had purchased the newspaper formerly owned by Joseph's brother, Albert, the *New York Journal,* and was trying to beat Pulitzer at his own game. Hearst imitated

An Amerian battleship, the Maine, *exploded in Havana Harbor on February 15, 1898. Although the cause of the explosion was not known, newspapers like Pulitzer's* New York World *and Hearst's* New York Journal *blamed Spain, and the United States started the Spanish American War.*

the *World* in nearly all aspects of its journalism: appeal to the masses, sensational stories, crusades.

The one way that Hearst did not imitate Pulitzer was in gathering news. The writers at the *Journal* waited until the morning edition of the *World* arrived and simply rewrote the articles for their evening paper. The *Journal* staff would chant,

Sound the cymbals, beat the drums;

The *World* is here, the news has come.

Pulitzer was wild with rage. Everything he did, Hearst did, and to add to the insult, Hearst hired Pulitzer's entire staff away—they all walked a block down the street to the *Journal* offices. Pulitzer hired them back, and they walked back. Hearst offered them still more money, and they left again. At this point Pulitzer gave up and searched for other editors and writers. Hearst even imitated a comic strip, called "The Yellow Kid," that ran in the *World*. The comic strip in the *Journal* actually had the same name: "The Yellow Kid." Some people think that it was from this title that the phrase *yellow journalism* began—it is a phrase used for tabloid newspapers that carry sensational stories but don't worry about whether they are true.

Hearst used the Cuban uprising against Spain as the pretext for gruesome stories of Spanish atrocities. The stories sold newspapers. Whether they were true or not did not interest Hearst. At first, Pulitzer's correspondents sent factual reports from Cuba, carefully researched and objectively written. These stories did not sell newspapers. The *Journal*'s circulation grew. The *World*'s circulation decreased. Pulitzer became more and more enraged until he was telling his writers to make their stories better—and by "better" he meant bloodier and more horrible. He was so determined to defeat Hearst that he forgot the principles of accuracy that he had upheld throughout his career. During this very difficult period in his life, Pulitzer's seventeen-year-old daughter Lucille died of typhoid.

Spain did not want a war with America. America did not want a war with Spain. But when an American battleship, the *Maine,* blew up in Havana Harbor, the two newspapers blamed it on the Spanish (who may have had nothing to do with the explosion), and the United States declared war. The American casualties were horrible: while about four hundred were actually killed in battle, more than five thousand died of malaria, typhoid, dysentery, and yellow fever.

Joseph Pulitzer deeply regretted the excesses his newspaper had committed during the war with Spain. He had lost the respect of the people whose opinion he most cared for, the honest journalists and politicians and intellectuals who knew he had abandoned his principles. Even though his war with Hearst for circulation caused him to condone practices he normally would not have allowed, it is important to realize that he was a very sick man at the time. His punishment was being branded a yellow journalist and considered to be no better than William Randolph Hearst.

The Columbia University School of Journalism, shown here, was created by Joseph Pulitzer's legacy and supervises the Pulitzer Prize awards each year.

THE PULITZER PRIZES

I n spite of his blindness and poor health, Joseph Pulitzer worked hard to raise the level of the *World.* He wanted to overcome the bad reputation of yellow journalism that the *World* had gained in its competition with Hearst's *Journal.* Pulitzer sent constant reminders to his editors to emphasize accuracy and penalized any stories that he felt were exaggerated for the sake of sensationalism. He wanted to see journalism respected as a profession, and to promote that he endowed Columbia University with $2 million for the establishment of the School of Journalism. Of this amount, $500,000 was to be used to establish awards for excellence in writing.

In May 1904, Pulitzer wrote an article in *The North American Review* urging the founding of a school of journalism: "Our Republic and its press will rise or fall together. An able, disinterested, public-spirited press, with trained intelligence to know the right and courage to do it, can preserve that public virtue without which popular government is a sham and a mockery."

At first Columbia was hesitant about accepting Pulitzer's endowment, but he finally prevailed. He stated, "I am deeply interested in the progress and elevation of journalism, having spent my life in that profession, regarding it as a noble profession and one of unequaled importance for its influence upon the minds and morals of the people. I desire to assist in attracting to this profession young men of character and ability, also to help those already engaged in the profession to acquire the highest moral and intellectual training."

At first Pulitzer had only considered forming a school for journalists. When he heard about the prizes that Alfred Nobel created, he thought they were a good idea. While the Nobel prizes concentrated on science and medicine, Pulitzer wanted his prizes to be for journalism and the arts. And while the Nobel prizes were for anyone in the world, Pulitzer wanted his prizes to be only for Americans.

Joseph Pulitzer died aboard his yacht *Liberty* in the harbor of Charleston, South Carolina, on October 29, 1911. The cause of death was listed as heart failure. One year later the Columbia School of Journalism was founded. The first Pulitzer Prizes were awarded in 1917 under the supervision of the advisory board at Columbia, which he had described in his will.

Pulitzer specified nine prizes: four in journalism, three in literature, one in drama, and one in essay writing. He was wise enough to realize that changes would occur over the years, so he gave the advisory board "power in its discretion to suspend or to change any subject or subjects, substituting, however, others in their places, if in the judgment of the board such suspension, changes, or substitutions shall be conducive to the public good or rendered advisable by public necessities, or by reason of change of time." He also gave the board the authority not to award a prize in any category if they felt there was no entry that met high enough standards.

The advisory board, renamed the Pulitzer Prize Board, has increased the number of awards over the years, has subdivided some categories and added others. There are currently twenty-one awards made each year. The journalism categories have been expanded and redefined. The prize for editorial cartoons was created in 1922. The prize for photography was begun in 1942 and in 1968 was divided into breaking news and feature photography. Of the twenty-one yearly awards, fourteen are for journalism.

Five awards are for books in the categories of fiction, history, biography, poetry, and nonfiction. The award for poetry was established in 1922, and the award for nonfiction in 1962. An award for music was begun in 1943. The board also may grant special awards and citations when it feels acknowledgment is due for a work or service that does not fit into one of the existing categories.

An elaborate process selects the people who receive the Pulitzer Prizes. If you would like to win a Pulitzer Prize, here's what you need to do:

How to Win a Pulitzer Prize in Journalism

First, of course, you must produce a work of high quality. You do not need to be a professional journalist or writer or photographer, however. Over the years several amateurs have won prizes, particularly in photography. You do need to have your work published in a United States newspaper that is published daily, Sunday, or at least once a week. Since most newspapers are glad to receive great photos, well-written articles, or guest editorials on important issues, your work has an excellent chance of being published if it's good.

Second, you must prepare and submit your entry application. Your entry needs to include a scrapbook, not larger than twelve by seventeen inches, containing your published work, with the name and date of the paper. You also need to submit a one- or two-page summary of your exhibit, and a biography and picture of yourself that will be used if you win a prize.

Each entry must include a completed entry form and a fifty-dollar entry fee. You can make the same entry in two categories, but not more than two. Entries must be received by February 1. The entry forms can be obtained by calling the Pulitzer Prize Office at (212) 854-3841, or online at www.pulitzer.org. Entries should be submitted to Pulitzer Prize Office, 709 Journalism, 2950 Broadway, Mail Code 3865, Columbia University, New York, NY 10027.

After your entry is received, along with the more than 2,000 other entries that are submitted each year, it will be given to the committee that will evaluate it. Early in March, the 102 appointed judges, who are editors, publishers, writers, and educators, get together in the Columbia University School of Journalism to make three nominations for each category. There will be at least five members on each committee. They spend three very intense days examining every entry. At the end of three days, they select three entries to nominate for the Pulitzer Prize in the category that they have been judging.

In early April the Pulitzer Prize Board gathers in the Pulitzer World Room of the Columbia School of Journalism, under a stained glass window depicting the Statue of Liberty that was taken from Joseph Pulitzer's *World* building. There are fifteen voting members on the board, including editors, reporters, and the president of Columbia University. The dean of the School of Journalism and the administrator of the board are nonvoting members. The members of the board have spent the weeks before this meeting reading the entries. The board has a lot of power. If it doesn't like any of the works nominated by the committee, it can ask the administrator to call the committee chairman to ask if there were any other good entries. If it still doesn't like any of the entries, the board can decide there will be no award given in a particular category that year. The Pulitzer Prize Board can also select an entry that was not nominated by the committee, or it can decide to switch a nomination from one category to another.

All of this activity by the committees and the board takes place in complete secrecy until the prizes are announced. This happens about a week after the meeting of the board in the World Room. The announcement of the prizes, made at 3:00 P.M., includes the name of the winner in each category and the names of the other two finalists. It is a great honor to be one of the three finalists, even if you do not win the prize.

Unlike the Nobel prize ceremonies, which are very formal and fancy, with banquets and gold medals and royal receptions and a lot of money for the winners, the Pulitzer Prize awards are very low key. Only one gold medal is awarded, for the winner in the Public Service category. The other winners get certificates and cash awards of $7,500. Instead of a royal banquet, the Pulitzer Prize winners have lunch in the rotunda of the Low Library at Columbia. The board has refused all offers to have the occasion be a big television show like the Academy Awards or other famous awards. They prefer the quiet and dignity that they feel Joseph Pulitzer would have wanted.

The main benefit that the Pulitzer Prize winners receive is not money or medals. It is the recognition of the excellence of their work, and the importance of their service in following the principles that Joseph Pulitzer followed for the greater part of his career. For example, more awards in journalism go to the exposure of corruption than to any other subject. It is for these awards for excellence in writing, and for public service and the cause of democracy, that Pulitzer is now remembered. He would be pleased.

Historical Epilogue: In 1931, Pulitzer's sons (Ralph, 1879-1939 and Joseph, 1885-1955) sold the New York papers to the Scripps-Howard chain and the *Evening World* was merged with the *New York Telegram.* The *St. Louis Post-Dispatch* was run by son Joseph and then by grandson Joseph (1913-1993). Today, grandson Michael E. Pulitzer (grandson Joseph's half-brother) is Chairman of the Board. Joseph's widow, Emily Pulitzer (Michael's sister-in-law) is also a director on the board. Day-to-day operations at the *Post-Dispatch* are handled by Terrance C. Z. Egger, publisher.

THE PULITZER PRIZE

Pulitzer Prize Winners 1998–2002 (For a complete listing of all Pulitzer Prizes, 1917–Present, see www.pulitzer.org/Archive/archive.html)

Journalism

Public Service
1998 *Grand Forks (N.D.) Herald*
1999 *Washington Post*
2000 *Washington Post*
2001 *Oregonian*
2002 *New York Times*

Breaking News Reporting
1998 Staff of *Los Angeles Times*
1999 Staff of *Hartford Courant*
2000 Staff of *Denver Post*
2001 *Miami Herald* Staff
2002 Staff of *Wall Street Journal*

Investigative Reporting
1998 Gary Cohn and Will Englund of *Baltimore Sun*
1999 Staff of *Miami Herald*
2000 Sang-Hun Choe, Charles J. Hanley and Martha Mendoza of *Associated Press*
2001 David Willman of *Los Angeles Times*
2002 Sari Horwitz, Scott Higham and Sarah Cohen of *Washington Post*

Explanatory Writing
1998 Paul Salopek of *Chicago Tribune*
1999 Richard Read of *Oregonian*
2000 Eric Newhouse of *Great Falls (Mont.) Tribune*
2001 *Chicago Tribune* Staff
2002 *New York Times* Staff

Beat Reporting
1998 Linda Greenhouse of *New York Times*
1999 Chuck Philips and Michael A. Hiltzik of *Los Angeles Times*
2000 George Dohrmann of *St. Paul Pioneer Press*
2001 David Cay Johnston of *New York Times*
2002 Gretchen Morgenson of *New York Times*

National Reporting
1998 Russell Carollo and Jeff Nesmith of *Dayton Daily News*
1999 Staff of *New York Times*, and notably Jeff Gerth
2000 Staff of *Wall Street Journal*
2001 *New York Times* Staff
2002 *Washington Post* Staff

International Reporting
1998 Staff of *New York Times*
1999 Staff of *Wall Street Journal*

2000   Mark Schoofs of *Village Voice*

2001   Ian Johnson of *Wall Street Journal;* Paul Salopek of *Chicago Tribune*

2002   Barry Bearak of *New York Times*

Feature Writing

1998   Thomas French of *St. Petersburg Times*

1999   Angelo B. Henderson of *Wall Street Journal*

2000   J.R. Moehringer of *Los Angeles Times*

2001   Tom Hallman, Jr., of *Oregonian*

2002   Barry Siegel of *Los Angeles Times*

Commentary

1998   Mike McAlary of *New York Daily News*

1999   Maureen Dowd of *New York Times*

2000   Paul A. Gigot of *Wall Street Journal*

2001   Dorothy Rabinowitz of *Wall Street Journal*

2002   Thomas Friedman of *New York Times*

Criticism

1998   Michiko Kakutani of *New York Times*

1999   Blair Kamin of *Chicago Tribune*

2000   Henry Allen of *Washington Post*

2001   Gail Caldwell of *Boston Globe*

2002   Justin Davidson of *Newsday,* Long Island, N.Y.

Editorial Writing

1998   Bernard L. Stein of *Riverdale (N.Y.) Press,* a weekly

1999   Editorial Board of *New York Daily News*

2000   John C. Bersia of *Orlando Sentinel*

2001   David Moats of *Rutland (Vt.) Herald*

2002   Alex Raksin and Bob Sipchen of *Los Angeles Times*

Editorial Cartooning

1998   Stephen P. Breen of *Asbury Park Press,* Neptune, N.J.

1999   David Horsey of *Seattle Post-Intelligencer*

2000   Joel Pett of *Lexington (Ky.) Herald-Leader*

2001   Ann Telnaes of *Los Angeles Times Syndicate*

2002   Clay Bennett of *Christian Science Monitor*

Spot/Breaking News Photography

1998   Martha Rial of *Pittsburgh Post-Gazette*

1999   Staff of *Associated Press*

2000   Photo Staff of *Denver Rocky Mountain News*

2001   Alan Diaz of *Associated Press*

2002 *New York Times* Staff

Feature Photography
1998 Clarence Williams of *Los Angeles Times*
1999 Staff of *Associated Press*
2000 Carol Guzy, Michael Williamson and Lucian Perkins of *Washington Post*
2001 Matt Rainey of *Star-Ledger*, Newark, N.J.
2002 *New York Times* Staff

Letters, Drama, and Music

Fiction
1998 *American Pastoral* by Philip Roth (Houghton Mifflin)
1999 *The Hours* by Michael Cunningham (Farrar, Straus and Giroux)
2000 *Interpreter of Maladies* by Jhumpa Lahiri (Mariner Books/Houghton Mifflin)
2001 *The Amazing Adventures of Kavalier & Clay* by Michael Chabon (Random House)
2002 *Empire Falls* by Richard Russo (Alfred A. Knopf)

Drama
1998 *How I Learned to Drive* by Paula Vogel
1999 *Wit* by Margaret Edson
2000 *Dinner With Friends* by Donald Margulies
2001 *Proof* by David Auburn

2002 *Topdog/Underdog* by Suzan-Lori Parks

History
1998 *Summer for the Gods: The Scopes Trial and America's Continuing Debate Over Science and Religion* by Edward J. Larson (BasicBooks)
1999 *Gotham: A History of New York City to 1898* by Edwin G. Burrows and Mike Wallace (Oxford University Press)
2000 *Freedom From Fear: The American People in Depression and War, 1929–1945* by David M. Kennedy (Oxford University Press)
2001 *Founding Brothers: The Revolutionary Generation* by Joseph J. Ellis (Alfred A. Knopf)
2002 *The Metaphysical Club: A Story of Ideas in America* by Louis Menand (Farrar, Straus and Giroux)

Biography or Autobiography
1998 *Personal History* by Katharine Graham (Alfred A. Knopf)
1999 *Lindbergh* by A. Scott Berg (G.P. Putnam's Sons)
2000 *Vera (Mrs. Vladimir Nabokov)* by Stacy Schiff (Random House)

2001 *W.E.B. Du Bois: The Fight for Equality and the American Century, 1919-1963* by David Levering Lewis (Henry Holt and Company)
2002 *John Adams* by David McCullough (Simon & Schuster)

Poetry
1998 *Black Zodiac* by Charles Wright (Farrar, Straus & Giroux)
1999 *Blizzard of One* by Mark Strand (Alfred A. Knopf)
2000 *Repair* by C. K. Williams (Farrar, Straus and Giroux)
2001 *Different Hours* by Stephen Dunn (W.W. Norton & Company)
2002 *Practical Gods* by Carl Dennis (Penguin Books)

General Nonfiction
1998 *Guns, Germs and Steel: The Fates of Human Societies* by Jared Diamond (W.W. Norton)
1999 *Annals of the Former World* by John McPhee (Farrar, Straus and Giroux)
2000 *Embracing Defeat: Japan in the Wake of World War II* by John W. Dower (W.W. Norton & Company/The New Press)
2001 *Hirohito and the Making of Modern Japan* by Herbert P. Bix (HarperCollins)

2002 *Carry Me Home: Birmingham, Alabama, the Climactic Battle of the Civil Rights Revolution* by Diane McWhorter (Simon & Schuster)

Music
1998 *String Quartet #2 (musica instrumentalis)* by Aaron Jay Kernis
1999 *Concerto for Flute, Strings and Percussion* by Melinda Wagner
2000 *Life Is a Dream, Opera in Three Acts: Act II, Concert Version* by Lewis Spratlan
2001 *Symphony No. 2 for String Orchestra* by John Corigliano
2002 *Ice Field* by Henry Brant

Special Citation
1998 George Gershwin, for his distinguished and enduring contributions to American music
1999 Duke Ellington, in recognition of his musical genius

CHRONOLOGY

1847	Born in Makó, Hungary, on April 10
1853	Pulitzer family moves to Budapest; Joseph educated by tutors
1864	Travels to America to join the Union Army
1865	Moves to St. Louis
1867	Becomes an American citizen
1869	Elected to the Missouri House of Representatives
1871	Becomes managing editor of the *Westliche Post*
1878	Marries Kate Davis; buys the *St. Louis Dispatch,* which becomes the *St. Louis Post-Dispatch*
1879	Son Ralph born
1880	Daughter Lucille Irma born
1882	Daughter Katherine Ethel born
1883	Buys the *New York World*
1884	Daughter Katherine Ethel dies of pneumonia
1885	Son Joseph Pulitzer Jr. born; raises money for pedestal for Statue of Liberty; serves for four months in the U.S. House of Representatives
1886	Daughter Edith born
1888	Daughter Constance born
1895	Son Herbert born; William Randolph Hearst buys the *New York Journal* and begins circulation war with the *World*
1897	Daughter Lucille dies of typhoid; the *World* contributes to U.S. war with Spain
1911	Dies in Charleston, South Carolina, on October 29
1912	Columbia School of Journalism, endowed by Pulitzer, is founded
1917	First Pulitzer Prizes are awarded
1931	Sons Ralph and Joseph sell New York papers to Scripps-Howard chain
2003	*St. Louis Post-Dispatch* still owned by the Pulitzer family, with grandson Michael E. as Chairman of the Board

EVENTS IN JOSEPH PULITZER'S LIFETIME

1846   Mexican American War begins

1849   California Gold Rush

1853   Crimean War begins

1860   Abraham Lincoln elected U.S. President

1861   American Civil War begins

1865   Civil War ends; Lincoln assassinated

1866   Cholera epidemic hits St. Louis

1868   First elevated section of New York's rapid transit system opens

1869   First transcontinental rail line completed

1874   Bridge across Mississippi River connects St. Louis with East St. Louis

1876   Alexander Graham Bell patents the telephone

1883   Brooklyn Bridge completed in New York

1886   Statue of Liberty dedicated

1889   Over 2,200 die in the Johnstown flood in Pennsylvania

1896   Nobel prizes established

1898   Spanish American War begins

1901   President McKinley assassinated

1904   New York City subway system opened

1906   San Francisco earthquake and fire destroy city

1908   Henry Ford introduces the Model T Ford

FURTHER READING

FOR YOUNG ADULTS:

Granberg, W. J. *The World of Joseph Pulitzer.* London, New York, Toronto: Abelard-
    Schuman, Ltd., 1965.

Whitelaw, Nancy. *Joseph Pulitzer and the New York World.* Greensboro, N.C.: Morgan
    Reynolds, Inc., 2000.

ON THE INTERNET:

The Chief: The Life of William Randolph Hearst
dir.salon.com/books/review/2000/06/06/nasaw/index.html

Columbia University, School of Journalism
www.jrn.columbia.edu

Joseph Pulitzer and the Pulitzer Prizes, by Seymour Topping   www.pulitzer.org/
History/history.html

The Pulitzer Prizes
www.pulitzer.org

Statue of Liberty Facts
www.endex.com/gf/buildings/liberty/libertyfacts.htm

WORKS CONSULTED:

Bates, J. Douglas. *The Pulitzer Prize.* New York: Birch Lane Press, 1991.

Brian, Denis. *Pulitzer: A Life.* New York: John Wiley & Sons, 2001.

Hohenberg, John. *The Pulitzer Diaries.* Syracuse, N.Y.: Syracuse University Press,
    1997.

Juergens, George. *Joseph Pulitzer and the New York World.* Princeton, New Jersey:
    Princeton University Press, 1966.

Nasaw, David. *The Chief: The Life of William Randolph Hearst.* Boston: Houghton
    Mifflin, 2000.

Pfaff, Daniel W. *Joseph Pulitzer II and The Post-Dispatch.* University Park, Pa.: The
    Pennsylvania University Press, 1991.

Swanberg, W. A. *Pulitzer.* New York: Charles Scribner's Sons, 1967.

For Researchers: About 20,000 items, personal papers and professional papers of Joseph
Pulitzer can be found in the Rare Book and Manuscript Library at Columbia University,
6th floor east, 535 West 114th Street, New York, NY 10027

GLOSSARY

anti-Semitism (ant-eye-SEM-it-izm) persecution, prejudice, or discrimination against Jews.

circulation (sir-cue-LAY-shun) the number of copies of a periodical sold in a given period; for example, the number of daily papers sold in a day or of weekly magazines sold in a week.

Confederacy (con-FED-er-ah-see) the Southern states that attempted to leave the United States to become a separate country, thus starting the American Civil War.

corruption (core-RUP-shun) the abuse of public trust by those in business or government for their own personal gain.

crusade (crew-SAYD) an energetic movement to remove an evil or to improve a situation.

editorial (ed-it-TOR-ee-al) an article in a newspaper that gives the opinions of the editor, publisher, or other writer.

extortion (ex-TOR-shun) the act of gaining something valuable (such as money) by force or illegal power.

immigrant (IM-mig-rent)someone who comes into a country in order to live there.

journalism (JUR-nal-izm) the profession of collecting news for, writing for, editing, or managing a newspaper.

legislature (LED-jis-lay-cher) a political body that can make or change laws in a state or country.

licentious (lie-SENT-shus) having disregard for strict rules of correctness.

Magyars (MAG-yarz) the warlike people who settled in Hungary in the ninth century.

robber baron (ROB-er BARE-un) one of the greedy businessmen in the 19th Century who owned railroads or steel mills or oil refineries and made millions of dollars while not paying their workers enough to live on.

sensationalism (sen-SAY-shun-ul-izm) in journalism, the practice of presenting dramatic and emotional material in order to sell newspapers.

slave-gang system (SLAYV-GANG SIS-tum) the use of large numbers of slaves to farm plantations (as opposed to the sharecropper system).

Union (YUNE-yun) the Northern states that fought in the American Civil War to prevent the South from leaving to form their own country.

yellow journalism (YELL-oh JUR-nal-izm) the use of sensationalism in reporting without regard for accuracy or truthfulness.

INDEX